Wait and See

Vivien Alcock

Illustrated by

Jill Bennett

A Belitha Press Book

MARILYN MALIN BOOKS
in association with ANDRE DEUTSCH

First published in Great Britain in 1986 by
Marilyn Malin Books in association with André Deutsch Ltd.
105 Great Russell Street, London WC1B 3LJ

Conceived, designed and produced by Belitha Press Ltd.
2 Beresford Terrace, London N5 2DH

ISBN 0 233 97952 2
Printed in Spain

Chapter 1

When Sally came out of school, she saw that her brother was upset. He was standing in the playground, and trying hard not to cry.

'What's the matter, Ben?' she asked.

'Nothing,' he said.

'Have they called you that rude name again?'

He nodded, and wiped his nose with his fingers.

'It's your own fault,' she said, 'you eat too many sweets. And buns. And cakes. You eat too much of everything.'

She was only telling him for his own good. She had to look after him. Their mother had said so. He was younger than she was.

'Mop up your face,' she said, and gave him her hanky. Sally always had a clean hanky. She was that sort of girl.

She looked at him and saw there was a bump in his pocket.

'I can help you,' she said. 'Would you like me to?'

'How?'

'Like this,' she said.

She put her hand in his pocket and took out a bar of chocolate – and ate it.

'There,' she said, with her mouth full. 'You look thinner already.'

'Do I really, Sally?' he asked.

'Yes,' she said.

She saw that his other pocket was flat. It was a pity. She would like to have helped him again.

'Will I be able to get through the railings into the magic garden?' Ben asked hopefully.

'Not yet,' she said, 'I'll have to help you a lot more.'

Ben had never been in the magic garden. He had not even seen it. It was hidden from the road by dark shrubs and iron railings. The gate was kept locked.

But if you were thin, you could squeeze through the railings and go into the garden. Sally was thin enough. All the other children in their street were thin enough. All except Ben.

Ben was as round as a football. He was almost as high when he was lying down as he was when he was standing up. To get him through the railings was like trying to post an elephant in a letterbox – impossible.

So he was left behind. He would stand like a prisoner, staring through the iron bars. When the other children came back, they told him the garden was magic.

'Poor Ben,' they said. 'You don't know what you're missing. It's magic.'

But they never told him any more.

'Is the garden really magic?' he asked Sally, as they walked home.

'Yes,' she said.

'How?' he asked.

'Ah,' she said, and smiled. 'Wait and see.'

'Will I really be able to get into it?' he asked.

'If I help you,' his sister said, 'if you do what I say. Only you mustn't tell Mum.'

'Why not?'

'Um – er – it would spoil things.'

She knew her mother liked Ben the way he was. Mum liked his round pink cheeks. She called him her 'roly-poly cherub' or 'cuddly-chops'. It made Sally sick.

She decided she would help Ben as much as possible. She liked to think she was a kind girl.

They went to tea with their grandmother that day. Gran had some Christmas cake left. Ben liked the icing best. He always saved it till last. So he put it to one side of his plate –

Sally snatched it and stuffed it into her mouth.

'Hey!' Ben cried angrily.

'I'm helping you,' Sally whispered. He saw his icing, yellow and white, churning around in her mouth. He remembered the magic garden.

'What's the matter, Ben?' Gran asked, turning round.

'Nothing,' he said sadly.

When they got home, Ben went up to their mother's room. He looked at himself in the long mirror. He looked at himself frontwards. He looked at himself sideways. He looked over his shoulder.

'What are you doing?' Sally asked, coming in to the room.

'I don't look any thinner to me,' he said. 'My tummy still sticks out.'

'Not so much. It stuck out to here before,' Sally said. She put her hand out to show him.

'Did it really?' he asked.

'Are you calling me a liar? If you don't want me to help you, just say so.'

'I do,' he said quickly. 'Please help me.'

'All right,' Sally said. She looked pleased. 'Only it's not easy, you know.

It's very kind of me to help you, isn't it?'

'Yes, Sally,' Ben said meekly.

That night he dreamed of the magic garden. There were silver fountains and golden fish that sang like birds. There was a white pony to ride, and a dragon as tame as a fat cat. There were swings and roundabouts, and a yellow car for him to drive.

Chapter 2

Sally went on helping him. She ate his buns. She ate his apple pie. She ate his cake. She ate his chocolate.

'Do I really look thinner?' he asked her every morning.

And every morning she said, 'Yes. Of course you do. I'm helping you, aren't I?'

'Then why do they still call me – you know what – at school?'

'Oh, they're silly,' Sally said. 'Don't take any notice of them.'

'But why do they?'

'You can't expect miracles,' Sally said. 'You *are* thinner, but only a little bit.'

'How much?' he asked.

'That much,' she said, and put her finger and thumb close together.

'You said that much before!' he said, holding his hands wide apart.

'I can't be expected to remember exactly,' she said crossly. 'If you don't want me to help you, just say so.'

Ben thought about it. He was always hungry now. He looked down at his tummy. It still stuck out. Then he saw something else.

'Sally! Sally!' he cried, jumping up and down, 'I can see over my tummy. I can see my feet now. I must be thinner.'

'I told you so,' she said smugly. 'If you keep on doing what I say, you'll soon be able to get into the magic garden.'

'Is it really magic, Sally?' he asked.

'Ah,' she said, and smiled. 'Wait and see.'

Chapter 3

On Saturday they were given their pocket money.

'You must give it to me,' Sally said, when they were outside.

'Why?'

'So that you can't buy any sweets, of course. I'm only trying to help you.'

'I won't buy sweets,' he promised. 'I'll save up and buy that model boat.'

Sally shook her head, and held out her hand.

'No. You must give it to me,' she said sternly. 'You know what you are. You'll go into the shop and see all those chocolate bars, and you won't be able to stop yourself. If you give your money to me, you can't be tempted, see?'

'Will you save it up for me and buy me that model boat?' he asked.

'Hand it over first and I'll tell you.'

He gave her his money. She put it in her pocket.

'Will you get me the model boat?' he asked.

'No,' she said.

'Give it back!' he cried, and tried to take it out of her pocket. She ran down the street, laughing. He ran after her.

But his legs were too short. He stopped. He was panting and red in the face.

'I hate you! You're a pig!' he shouted.

'I'm only helping you,' she shouted back. 'Don't you want me to help you any more, Ben? Don't you want to be able to go into the magic garden?'

'How does it help me to take my money?' he asked bitterly.

'It made you run after me,' Sally said, coming back to him. 'You see? Running is good for you. It shakes the fat off.'

'Does it really?' he asked.

'Yes,' Sally said, and jingled the money in her pocket.

'Can I have my money back, then?'

'No,' she said, 'it would spoil the magic.'

'Why?' he asked.

'Um – er – because I say so,' Sally said. She went skipping down the street. Her mother was right. It did make you feel good to help other people.

Chapter 4

Every day after school, Ben looked through the railings of the magic garden. All he could see were the big, dark bushes. Sometimes he could hear children laughing but he could not see them. He tried to squeeze through, but it was no good. He was still too fat.

'How long will it take, Sally?' he asked her one day.

'Not long,' she said. 'Give me a push, Ben.'

Ben pushed her, and she popped through the railings like a cork out of a bottle.

'Can't you push me through?' he begged.

'Not yet,' she said, and ran off into the bushes.

Ben was left outside. He sniffed.

He was hungry. He never had any sweets now, or cake or ice-cream. He didn't even have his pocket money to

save up for his model boat. Sally took
it all.

He looked at the dark, shiny leaves,
and wondered what it was like in the
magic garden. None of the other children
ever told him. They just said, 'It's magic.
You don't know what you're missing,
Ben.'

He put his left leg and his left arm through the railings. He pushed. He shoved. The railings dug into his stomach. They dug into his bottom.

He was going through! Bit by bit. Going, going – stuck!

Now he couldn't go backwards or forwards. He was held fast like a nut in a pair of nutcrackers.

'Sally!' he screamed. 'Sally!'

He could hear children laughing in the garden. But Sally did not come.

'Sally!' he screamed again.

Then he heard footsteps on the pavement. He looked round.

Two men were walking towards him. They were laughing. He hated them.

'Got yourself stuck, have you, son?' the tall man said.

'Don't see how we can get you out,' the short one said. 'Have to call the Fire Brigade. They can saw through the railing.'

'Pity to spoil good railings,' the tall one said. 'If we leave him for a few days, he will get thin enough to come out by himself.'

Ben thought about it. He thought of the night and the dark and the owls in the trees. He began to cry.

The two men were sorry.

'We were only teasing, son,' they said. 'We'll get you out all right.'

They took hold of the iron bars and tried to bend them apart. They puffed. They panted. Their faces went red. Beads of sweat sparkled on their foreheads.

'It's no good,' the short man said at last, 'the bars are too strong.'

'I know,' the tall one said. 'Wait a moment. I'll get some oil from my car.'

He came back carrying a can of oil.

'It's going to mess up your coat, son,' he said. 'I hope your mum won't be cross. Perhaps we had better call the Fire Brigade after all.'

'No,' Ben said. 'Please get me out.'

The man poured the oil over Ben. It ran down his coat, thick and yellow. It ran down his trousers, thick and sticky. It ran into his shoes.

'One, two, three – PULL!' the short man cried.

Ben slid out of the railings like a
sardine from a tin. He stood on the
pavement, dripping oil and tears.

'I'll never try again,' he said. 'I'm
going to eat all the sweets and cakes I
want. I won't give Sally my pocket money
any more. I hate the garden! I don't
believe it's magic. I don't believe in
magic any more.'

The tall man was wiping Ben down with a rag.

'Now, now,' he said. 'Can't have that. Who is this Sally?'

'My sister,' Ben said. He told the men all about Sally helping him.

'She eats all your sweets and cakes and pudding?' the tall man asked.

'Yes. Just to help me.'

'I see. And what is this about your pocket money?'

Ben told him.

'What does she do with your money?' the short man asked. 'Is she saving it up for you?'

'No. She said it would spoil the magic.'

'Oh, she did, did she? So what does she spend it on?'

'She buys sweets.'

'Sweets?'

'It's just to help me,' Ben explained, 'She says she doesn't really like them. But she wants to show me how horrid they are. So she eats them in front of me, saying things like – "Yuk! Poo! Horrible!" all the time.'

'I see,' the tall man said, and laughed. 'I'd like to meet Miss Sally. She's a sly one, if you ask me. But she's got it coming to her.'

'What?' Ben asked, puzzled.

'Ah,' the man said, 'you wait and see.'

'Don't you worry, son,' the short man said. 'There's magic and magic. Don't ever stop believing that.'

Chapter 5

'What have you done to your coat, Ben?'
his mother asked him later.

'Nothing.'

'What do you mean "nothing"? It's
filthy! I do think you might take care
of –' She stopped and looked at his face.

'What's the matter, love?' she asked
softly.

'Nothing.'

'Has Sally been teasing you?'

'No.'

'Don't you feel well?'

'Yes. I'm all right.'

'Go and change your clothes, Ben,' his mother said. 'Then you can have some milk. And a slice of cake.'

'I don't want any cake, thanks, Mum.'

'No cake?'

'No,' he said. 'I don't feel like it.'

'You must be sickening for something,' his mother said, looking anxious. 'Go to bed, and I'll bring you up some chicken soup.'

When she came up to his room, she sat by his bed. Ben drank the chicken soup. Then he said, 'Mum, you know the big garden behind the railings?'

'You mean the garden of the old manor house? Yes, I do,' she said.

'Is it really magic?'

His mother smiled. Her eyes were dreamy.

'I used to go there when I was a girl,' she said. 'They had parties in the garden. In summer, they put candles in jam-jars and hung them in the trees. Ever so pretty it was.'

'But is it magic?'

'I thought so then,' his mother said.

Ben looked at her. She was looking young and pink and pretty.

'What about now?' he asked. 'Is it still magic now?'

'Well, the house is empty and locked up,' his mother said. 'I don't think you can get into the garden. Pity. I'd love to see it again.'

'I'm going to see it,' Ben said. 'One day.'

Chapter 6

So he let Sally go on helping him. He gave her his pocket money. He passed her his cake under the table. He let her swipe his ice-cream off his plate, when their mother was not looking. But he never went to look through the railings into the magic garden any more.

A new girl came to their school. She had black curly hair and bright eyes. Ben thought she was beautiful.

'Have a sweet?' she said one day. She held out a bag.

'No thanks,' he said.

'I eat too many sweets,' she said. 'If I don't look out, I'll be fat.'

Ben blushed. He thought she was being horrible.

'If you call me that name,' he said, 'I'll hit you.'

She stared at him. 'What do you mean?
What name?'

'You know.'

'No, I don't.'

'What the other kids call me,' he said,
his face red.

'They call you Ben,' she said. 'That's
your name, isn't it?'

'Yes,' he said, 'but they don't call me
Ben. They call me . . .' He did not want
to say it aloud. Fatso, that's what they

called him. Fatso.

'Hey, Ben!' a boy called. 'Come and play football with us!'

'Yes, come on, Ben!' another boy shouted.

'You're batty,' the pretty girl said. 'You don't know your own name.'

Ben went to play football. Nobody called him Fatso. They called him Ben. When had they last called him Fatso? He did not remember.

Chapter 7

After tea, he and Sally went out.

'I'm going to play in the magic garden,' Sally said.

'So am I,' Ben said.

'You're not ready yet,' Sally told him. 'I'll have to help you a lot more. Don't

forget to give me your pocket money on Saturday.'

They came to the railings. Ben looked at them. Funny. They seemed wider apart.

Sally tried to squeeze through.

'Push me, Ben,' she said.

Ben pushed.

'Harder, Ben!'

Ben pushed harder.

'Ow! Stop!' she cried. 'It hurts.'

She kicked the railings.

'What's the matter with them?' she said.

'It's not them. It's you,' Ben said.

'You're too fat. You helped me too much, Sally.'

He slid through the railings and ran into the bushes.

'You're silly!' Sally screamed after him. 'It isn't magic at all! It's just a stupid old garden!'

Sally waited. She felt bad. She was fond of Ben in her way. She wished she had not told him the garden was magic. Now he would be disappointed. He would be cross with her for telling lies. He might tell Mum about his pocket money. Then Mum would be cross with her too.

'I was only trying to help,' she mut-

tered. She blew her nose in her hanky.

Two men walked by. One was tall and the other was short.

'Can't you get into the magic garden?' the tall man asked.

'It's not magic,' Sally said angrily. 'It's not magic at all.'

'Ah, that's what you think,' the short one said, 'but we know better. There's magic and magic.'

'You'll have to ask your brother to help you now,' the tall man said.

Then they laughed and walked on.

Sally waited again. At last Ben came back.

'I'm sorry, Ben,' Sally mumbled. 'I was only trying to help.'

Then she saw his face. It was as bright
as a Christmas candle. His eyes shone.

Sally stared at him. Why did he look
so happy? Had he found something in the
garden that she had missed?

'What's happened, Ben? Why do you
look so pleased?' she asked. 'Is the garden
really magic after all?'

'Ah,' Ben said and smiled. 'Wait and
see.'